*This copy combining only straight lines, is intended as an exercise producing a fr[...]
with the hand sliding on the nails of the 3rd and 4th fingers. Lines unite at top and bas[...]
this book, combinations should begin at lower left corner, be written through with continuous motion, [...]*

The diagrams found on pages 2 and 3 are designed to show how the letters are to be adjusted to the ruling.

This copy (*i, u* and *w*) combines First (**/**) and Second (**)**)Prin- ciples. The Second unites angularly with First at the top. Dot the *i* one space above its top on the regular slant. Finish *w* with a small dot, and Second Principle in horizontal position. Write the letters excepting *r* and *s* within the narrow spaces. *Caution: avoid unlike turns, thus* **ии**; *unequal spacing, thus***ии**; *different slants, thus* **ии**. *Count 1, 2, 1, 2, 1, 2, 3, 4, 1, 2, 3, 4, 5, dot 1, dot, dot.*

The *n* combines Principles 3, 1, 3, 1, 2. Turns alike at top and base. The curve connecting *u* with *n* is formed from a combination of Second and Third Principles, and is called a compound curve. Wherever it connects letters, the distance between the straight lines is one and one-third spaces. Write lightly. Different slants make the word appear, thus *nun*. Count 1, 2, 3, 4, 1, 2, 3, 4, 1.

nun nun nun nun nun nun 3

4

For full explanation of figures see second page of cover.

*The **m** combines Principles 3, 1, 3, 1, 3, 1, 2. Straight lines parallel and equally spaced. Curve lines same length and slant. Dot the **i** after the combination is written. In **i** and **u** avoid uniting the Second and First Principles too low down, thus $\mathcal{uu}$; or rounding their tops, thus $\mathcal{nn}$. Count 1, 2, 3, 4, 5, 6, 1, 2, 1, 2, 3, 4, 1 dot.*

miu miu miu miu miu miu 4

Turn in **n**, **x** and **v**, at top and base the same, i.e., as short as possible with continuous motion. The **x** combines Principles 3, 1, 2, 1. The **v** combines 3, 1, 2, 2. After the combination is written, finish **x** by beginning at the base line, crossing upward through middle of First Principle, with a straight line, on the same slant with curves, and ending at upper line. Finish **v** same as **w**. Count 1, 2, 3, 4, 1, 2, 1, 2, 1, 2, 3, dot 1, cross, cross.

In the even numbered copies throughout the book, except copy 8 the 1st, 3rd and 5th down strokes at top touch the upper and vertical lines, i.e. appear in corners, as per diagram page 2. Small o formed by a union of Principles 3, 3, 1, width one-third of length. Opposite sides equally curved and closed at top. The o's joined with Second Principle in horizontal position. Avoid the full curve at the left side, thus ∂ . Count 1, 2, 3, etc.

000000 000000 000000 000000 000000 000000 6

The ruling of the odd numbered copies at the beginning of the combinations, regulates the spacing, height, and slant of the letter or its first part as per diagram page 3. The letters must always touch upper and lower lines, commencing and ending in corners. Turns at top and base are one-sixth of a space.   Count 1, 2, 3, 4, 1, 2, 1, 2, 3, 4, 5, 6, 1, dot.

nim nim nim nim nim nim 7

The *a* combines Principles 3, 3, 2, 1, 2.

The Third Principle joins the oval one-fourth space from the upper line, measured vertically. Give the oval an increased inclination and unite to Second and First Principles at top.

Make the First Principles on regular slant. Avoid too full curves, thus *a* ; leaving *a* open at top, thus *a* ; a loop at top, thus *a* . Count 1, 2, 3, 4, 1, etc.

aaa aaa aaa aaa aaa aaa   8

*Straight lines equally spaced, except between **i** and **m**, where the compound curve occurs, which increases the distance one-third space. Avoid unlike slants in straight lines, thus **aim**; lifting the pen between letters and parts of letters, thus **aim**. Count 1, 2, 3, 4, 1, 2, 1, 2, 3, 4, 5, 6, 1, dot.*

aim aim aim aim aim aim 9

For complete analysis see "Theory of Spencerian Penmanship."
The *e* combines Principles 2, 3, 2, Loop two-thirds the length. Left curve same as in *c* and *o*. Spaces equal. Avoid too full curves, thereby producing too large loops, thus 𝓵𝓵 ; too much slant, thus 𝓵𝓵. Stamp improvement upon every line. Count 1, 2, 1, 2, etc.

With careful movement write words without lifting the pen. Make the letters high enough to fill the spaces between the ruled lines.
Each pupil should have a correct mental conception of the form of every letter. Count 1, 2, 3, 4, 5, 6, 1, 2, 1, 2, 3, 4, 1.

men men men men men men 1

*The **c** combines Principles 2, 1, 2, 3, 2. Oval turn at top occupies one-third space. Loop two-thirds its height same as in **e**. Spaces equal. Avoid too large oval at top,*
thus ℒ ; a round back, thus ℒ ; a straight back, thus ℒ . Count 1, 2, 3, 4, 1, & repeat.

cccccc cccccc cccccc cccccc cccccc cccccc cccccc 2

*Observe carefully the oval top of **c**; the increased slant of pointed oval in **a**: the double curve connecting **a** and **m**. Pupils should form the habit of constantly criticizing their writing. Count 1, 2, 3, 4, 1, 2, 3, 4, 1, 2, 3, 4, 5, 6, 1.*

cam cam cam cam cam cam 3

The r combines Principles 2, 1, 2. Rise one and one-fourth spaces with Second Principle; drop downward with a slightly curved shoulder, and connect with First Principle. Avoid giving too much width to the r, thus ⋏ ; too full curve to the shoulder, thus ⋏ ; making loop, thus ⋏ . Count 1, 2, 3, & repeat.

4

*Straight lines equally distant except between **i** and **n**. Be careful to make the **r** of proper height and width. Avoid giving too much slant to its first curve, thus ✎;*
or making sharp shoulder, thus ✎ . Count 1, 2, 3, 1, 2, 3, 4, 1, 2, 1, 2, 3, 4, 1, dot.

ruin ruin ruin ruin ruin ruin 5

The s combines Principles 2, 3, 2, 3; commences and finishes with **r** curve. Occupies one and one-fourth spaces in height. Its dot rests on the first curve one-fourth space above the ruled line. Never loop it at top, thus 𝓁 ; or make it too wide, thus 𝓵 . Count 1, 2, 3 dot & repeat.

Count for some 1, 2, 3 dot 1, 2, 3, 4, 1, 2, 3, 4, 5, 6, 1.
Notice the joining of s with o, and of o with m. Dot s in proper place and close o at top. Think, think and write. Count 1, 2, 3, dot 1, 2, 3, 1, 2, 3, 4, 5, 6, 1, 2, 1.

some some some sum sum sum 7

18

The t combines Second and First Principles. The First Principle occupies two spaces in height and is on the regular slant.
The Second Principle joins First one space from base line. Cross it one-third its length from the top with a straight hairline, in horizontal position and in length, equal to
one space. Caution: Avoid unlike turns, thus 𝓾𝒾; different slants, thus 𝓾𝓽 . Count 1, 2, 3, 4, 1, 2, 1, 2, 3, 4, 1, 2, 1, cross, dot.

utui utui utui utui utui utui 8

The **d** combines Principles 3, 3, 2, 1, 2. First part like **a**. Finish like **t** without cross. Do not slant First Principle in **d** too much, thus *d* ; or make pointed oval too flat on the left side, thus *d* . Avoid unlike slants in First Principles, thus *dim*. Count 1, 2, 3, 4, 1, 2, 1, 2, 3, 4, 5, 6, 1 dot.

dim dim dim dim dim dim 9

*In **m** Third Principle unites with First angularly at base. Avoid grasping the pen too tightly. Count 1, 2, 3, 4, 5, 6, 1, 2, 1, 2, 3, 4, 5, dot 1.*

mew mew mew mew mew mew 0

Make true curves, and smooth straight lines, which will give a neat appearance. Count 1, 2, 3, 4, 5, 6, 1, 2, 3, 4, 1, 2, 1, cross.

max max max max max max 1

22

Criticise your own work. Be sure you are right, then go ahead. Count 1, 2, 3, 4, 5, 6, 1, 2, 1, 2, 3, 4, 1, 2, 1, dot.

miel miel miel miel miel miel 2

I gain every time I take pains with my line. Diligence ensures success. Count 1, 2, 3 dot 1, 2, 3, 4, 1, 2, 1, 2, 3, 4, 1, dot.

vain vain vain vain vain vain 3

Decided effort will make your last page the best. Adopt the motto—"I will strive to excel,"—and improvement is sure. Count 1, 2, 3, 4, 5, 6, 1, 2, 1, 2, 3, 1, 2, 1.

mere mere mere mere mere mere 4